MONSTERS!

BIGFOOT

BY FRANCES NAGLE

Gareth Stevens
PUBLISHING

Please visit our website, www.garethstevens.com. For a free color catalog of all our high-quality books, call toll free 1-800-542-2595 or fax 1-877-542-2596.

Cataloging-in-Publication Data

Names: Nagle, Frances.
Title: Bigfoot / Frances Nagle.
Description: New York : Gareth Stevens Publishing, 2016. | Series: Monsters! | Includes index.
Identifiers: ISBN 9781482448559 (pbk.) | ISBN 9781482448573 (library bound) | ISBN 9781482448566 (6 pack)
Subjects: LCSH: Sasquatch--Juvenile literature.
Classification: LCC QL89.2.S2 N335 2016 | DDC 001.944--dc23

First Edition

Published in 2017 by
Gareth Stevens Publishing
111 East 14th Street, Suite 349
New York, NY 10003

Designer: Samantha DeMartin
Editor: Kristen Nelson

Photo credits: Cover, p. 1 (background) isak55/Shutterstock.com; cover, p.1 (Bigfoot) BestGreenScreen/Shutterstock.com; pp. 5, 15 Grambo Grambo/First Light/Getty Images; p. 7 Rich Legg/E+/Getty Images; p. 9 flickr.com/photos/jenniferboyer/10894058315 (CC BY-ND 2.0); p. 11 Globe Turner/Shutterstock.com; p. 13 Popperfoto/Popperfoto/Getty Images; p. 17 flickr.com/photos/wiccked/52932187 (CC BY-NC-ND 2.0); p. 19 Fiziker/ Wikimedia Commons; p. 21 (drawing) Barcroft/Barcroft Media/Getty Images; p. 21 (paper) Bohbeh/Shutterstock.com; p. 23 Andrew Rich/Vetta/Getty Images; p. 25 Bill O'Leary/The Washington Post/Getty Images; p. 27 Darlene Hammon/Archive Photos/Getty Images; p. 29 David Muir/Photographer's Choice/Getty Images.

Printed in the United States of America

CPSIA compliance information: Batch #CS16GS: For further information contact Gareth Stevens, New York, New York at 1-800-542-2595.

CONTENTS

MONSTER ON THE LOOSE!

Imagine being out in the woods as the sun starts to set. Something moves nearby. It seems to follow you. Then, a rock hits a tree near you. You might be in the forest with Bigfoot!

BEYOND THE MYTH

The study and search for **mythical** monsters and beings is called cryptozoology.

5

Bigfoot is often called Sasquatch, which means "wild man." It's said to be a smelly, hairy **creature** that looks like a mix of a human and an ape. Reports say it's between 6 and 15 feet (1.8 and 4.6 m) tall!

BEYOND THE MYTH

Sasquatch is said to live in the northwestern United States and western Canada.

MAN OR BEAST?

Stories about Bigfoot haven't always been what they are today. Many Native American **cultures** believe Bigfoot is real. The Lakota people call Bigfoot "Chiye-tanka." In Lakota, "Chiye" means "older brother" and "tanka" means "big."

BEYOND THE MYTH

According to Native American myths, Bigfoot is on the border of being animal and being human, which makes him have a special power!

9

YETI

The Yeti myth likely started in Tibet, China. As far back as 326 BC, tales were told of a huge, humanlike monster in the Himalayan Mountains. In fact, Alexander the Great asked to see one when he was taking over the area!

BEYOND THE MYTH

The government in Nepal started giving out Yeti-hunting **licenses** in the 1950s! They offered money for any Yetis brought in. No one ever caught one, though.

•TIBET

HIMALAYAS

NEPAL•

THE YETI'S RANGE

11

The Yeti is said to live high in the mountains in the snow. Sightings aren't reported often. In 1921, a writer called it the **"Abominable** Snowman," a name that's stuck in movies and stories about the Yeti.

BEYOND THE MYTH

Bears have likely caused the huge "Yeti footprints" found in the Himalayas. When a bear steps forward, its back footprint will partly cover the footprint of the front foot, making it look larger.

13

ALMAS

The "wild man," or Almas, sounds a lot like Bigfoot and the Yeti. Stories say it lives in the mountains of central Asia and Mongolia. But the hairy Almas is believed to be just one of a group of wild people living out there!

BEYOND THE MYTH

One scientist thought the Almas and Sasquatch might be the last Neanderthals, the group of humans who lived on Earth about 100,000 to 300,000 years ago.

15

WORLDWIDE MONSTER

Stories about huge, humanlike monsters can be found in many other places around the world. In Australia, it's called the Yowie. In China, it's known as the Yeren, and in Scotland, it's the Ferles Mor.

BEYOND THE MYTH

Modern stories of the Yowie are based on the myths of the Aborigines, the native people of Australia. In their stories, the Yowie, or Yaroma, can't get its feet wet!

17

NO WAY!

Most scientists don't believe Bigfoot—or any of these other creatures—**exists**. They wonder what creatures that big would eat and how they could keep up their numbers. However, that doesn't stop people from reporting sightings!

BEYOND THE MYTH

Bigfoot sightings have been reported in every US state except Hawaii.

REPORTED BIGFOOT SIGHTINGS

459

0

CANADA

UNITED STATES

MEXICO

19

SIGHTINGS

Spotting something that looks like Bigfoot is easy. Proving you've seen it is hard! In 1811, David Thompson found what might have been the first set of footprints that could have been from Bigfoot. He couldn't prove it, though!

BEYOND THE MYTH

Most people who report Bigfoot sightings have no **evidence** to offer, only their memory!

21

The most famous Bigfoot sighting happened in 1967. Two men from Washington State caught a black, hairy creature on video. They'd been looking for Bigfoot for years. No one has been able to say for sure if their "evidence" was a **hoax**.

BEYOND THE MYTH

Many websites have the 1967 video. Do you think it's real? Check out: *http://www.oregonbigfoot.com/patterson.php.*

23

SEARCHING FOR BIGFOOT

There's no certain evidence that Bigfoot is real. Cryptozoologists are on the lookout for some, though. In addition, many people spend time trying to find footprints or catch Bigfoot on camera!

BEYOND THE MYTH

People search for other mythical creatures, or cryptids, too. The chupacabra is a doglike creature said to drink farm animals' blood!

A REPORTED BIGFOOT FOOTPRINT CAST

25

BIGFOOT ON THE BIG SCREEN

Could you imagine a friendly Bigfoot? In 1987, the movie *Harry and the Hendersons* did! A Bigfoot-like creature named Harry becomes a family friend. The movie was so popular, there was a TV show of the same name, too.

HARRY AND THE HENDERSONS

BEYOND THE MYTH

At the end of *Harry and the Hendersons*, Harry goes to find more creatures like himself. That might be the scary part of the story!

Many Bigfoot movies are a bit scary. There are many about Bigfoot or the Yeti (or Abominable Snowman) hurting people in the woods. They go after people looking for them, too. Perhaps these monsters don't want to be found!

BEYOND THE MYTH

The TV show *Finding Bigfoot* tries to do just that—discover evidence that Bigfoot is real!

SASQUATCH
CROSSING

29

Recent Bigfoot Sightings

WINLOCK, WA
November 2012

GREGORY COUNTY, SD
November 2006

KALKASKA COUNTY, MI
July 2014

BERKSHIRE COUNTY, MA
September 2015

LAS VEGAS, NM
October 2013

TUSCALOOSA COUNTY, AL
April 2014

FOR MORE INFORMATION

BOOKS

Anderson, Holly Lynn. *Unexplained Monsters and Cryptids.* Pittsburgh, PA: Eldorado Ink, 2015.

Baltzer, Rochelle. *Monsters and Other Mythical Creatures.* Minneapolis, MN: Magic Wagon, 2015.

Rivkin, Jennifer. *Searching for Bigfoot.* New York, NY: PowerKids Press, 2015.

WEBSITES

Finding Bigfoot: The Game
discoverykids.com/games/finding-bigfoot/
Play a game as Bigfoot, trying to escape people looking for you!

Top 10 Bigfoot Sightings of the Last 5 Years
animalplanet.com/tv-shows/finding-bigfoot/lists/10-bigfoot-sightings-last-5-years/
Read about people who think they've seen Bigfoot recently.

Publisher's note to educators and parents: Our editors have carefully reviewed these websites to ensure that they are suitable for students. Many websites change frequently, however, and we cannot guarantee that a site's future contents will continue to meet our high standards of quality and educational value. Be advised that students should be closely supervised whenever they access the Internet.

GLOSSARY

abominable: disagreeable

creature: an animallike being

culture: the beliefs and ways of life of a group of people

evidence: something that shows the truth of a story

exist: to have actual life or being

hoax: an act meant to trick someone into believing something that isn't true

license: a piece of paper that allows someone to do something

mythical: like a legend or story

INDEX